A Strange Relief

A Strange Relief

Poems by

SONNET L'ABBÉ

M&S

National Library of Canada Cataloguing in Publication Data

L'Abbé, Sonnet
A strange relief

ISBN 0-7710-4583-2

I. Title.

PS8573.A156S77 2001   C811'.6   C00-933044-5
PR9199.3.L22S77 2001

We acknowledge the financial support of the Government of
Canada through the Book Publishing Industry Development
Program for our publishing activities. We further acknowledge the
support of the Canada Council for the Arts and the Ontario Arts
Council for our publishing program.

Typeset in Bembo by M&S, Toronto
Printed and bound in Canada

McClelland & Stewart Ltd.
The Canadian Publishers
481 University Avenue
Toronto, Ontario
M5G 2E9
www.mcclelland.com

1 2 3 4 5   05 04 03 02 01

to my parents
and
to Jerome

CONTENTS

CHEJU DIARY

HIATUS

Lesson from the Neolithic Era

"Pottery can still be made without resort to science."
— Bernard Charles

Clay is an eternal experiment
in the quiet laboratory
of the ocean. The planet's
every pore still breathes clay, as it has since birth,
long before an electron eye
saw the micronic dimension of porcelain,
not colloidal, but particulate.

The salt sea is proof
of the dissolution of incalculable quantities of rock,
moon-drawn bath of continents.

We owe this raw material
to water's mechanical persuasion,
its abrasive persistence: the temperamental ocean wished
a fresh new floor from earth's
feldspathic crust, and disguised as rain
convinced igneous rock into slow submerged beds,
until a geologic argument, gradual as the fall
out of love, heaved these metamorphic strata
back to land, where they would patiently wait
for a potter's deeper desire.

The poetry of pottery is scientific,
hidden in the nomenclature of clay.
Listen to this.
Hydrous silicate of alumina.

Apology

Once I believed in the laws of motion.
My ignorant hands held all passed down as true:
progress, history's noble direction,

art's persistence – a buoy upon time's waves,
nodding and rolling in disturbed waters,
but grounded, a beacon, heaven-lit to save

us from ourselves – and likened my bodies of clay,
pulled upward from a spinning wheel,
to those first two bodies born, on the sixth day,

between God's own muddy fingers, His
inspired dirt moulded on the planet's turning
table. My faith met with no equal or opposed

forces: sure of my likeness to the Creator, the tools
of metal and of mind, sifted down through strata
of mentor and student, the craft's rules

and exceptions, were teachings as old
as that first moment, and I was one of the descended
few, to whom their endless inertia was trusted.

If once we dragged ourselves out of the sea, sand
ground our fins to limbs: before breathing,
we had first to clutch at land. We could not stand

before we crawled and smelled earth. Then pottery!
A handspring, an evolution, said those
who had dug and named the artifacts of history:

a revolutionary knowledge, this marriage
of all four elements, a bridge between two
eras, momentous enough to name an age

after these bisqued proofs of civilization,
now enshrined behind museums' glass. Who could argue
with the dead? Earth unearthed, they rose again

onto pedestals, their sunken vessels older
than bones. Let others leave behind
a tangled mess of children's children, I would throw

forward, to the coming time. I desired
another afterlife, not earned on a pew, pressing air
between my palms, but one born in the kiln's fire.

But I was a fault, the crack where one small quake
restacks the planet's plates, and throws askew
the buried, once unbroken, vein of clay – the weak

joint in tradition's fragile backbone. It took
so little, nothing spectacular, nothing geographic,
to shake me. Perhaps I looked

for my reward on Earth. From windworn pebbles
I never meant to pan for gold, only dust enough
to build a studio of bricks – no marble

columns, no limestone stairs – just walls
to keep the wolves away. They blew
it down, all of it, my spinning wheel stalled

and idle, in a hole, a gash of borrowed mud.
Caught in their machine, its turning cogs
greased with numbers. I could

not match silicon's new speed, debt's relentless
movement. So have I been ground down,
to ash dust on my shelves, to this motionless

body. So have I failed where God tested.
In this, there may be virtue still:
on the seventh day, even He rested.

A Lesson from Leach

"Come down. You are a potter's son."

There is a hierarchy of shape.
We are ever inside systems, neutral elusive,
but from stars' slow progress we can prove
ellipses know something we have yet to learn.

The potter suspects a code, a cryptic so well kept
our gathered remnants shout it,
a liquid, public skeleton
spilled off the porcelain lips of all perfection,
but you could listen your whole life
and never hear, as you must this language of land,
                              with your hands.

The secret of beauty is all around us.
We walk over it, staining our soles with earth.

Books might try to mould a curve, a sturdy foot,
but words cannot teach texture.
A vase, a vessel, is more perfect than geometry.
Realize this: a circle is describable.

Weight is learned by holding, feeling
the exact urgency of the earth as it asks
for its body back.
The shape of the blue orb's longing
thrown again and again, subtle as trust,
little planets born from the spinning wheel.
The wheel knows the centrifugal mind
of the universe, returning perennially to form.

A poem about pots is colour to the blind.
This theory of mine holds water.

7

Night Vision

His wife dreams of silent flight.

On a drive on narrow roads
outside the city
she points to the red horizon,
where the sun, a hydrogen zeppelin,
skin aflame, lingers
inflated and floating along the highway,
as black silhouettes of balloons
rise with the moon
into the flushed sky.

Look, she says, *twilight wears
a necklace of weightless onyx tears,
the moon a pendant, opal planet.*

He replies that to him
they are round-bellied bottles,
necks down, poured out,
and hollow.
Baskets cling to their pouted lips
like drops of liquor,
drips of euphoria tinged
with fear, last sips
of liquid altitude, from where
one looks upon this vastness
and sees the flat horizon's curve.

Must you see pots in everything?
Her sigh, the hush of fire.

But he has lied.
What he really sees tonight

are question marks
in their distant outlines, doubled
and considering their own reflections,
a darkness inside them empty
as the negative goblet
of space between two facing profiles.
They are wondering
how we travel so far
on warm wordless breaths,
and asking themselves
who they are.

A Lesson from Hamada

Distant student,
myself and Leach do watch
your worship, through you
unburied, burned, and reborn.

Our heir, you wear
a soft glitter of ash,
rough crown of dust,
the rhythmic kick, kick
of your foot on the kickwheel
steady as a march.

You share our courts:
cellar studio, its musty air.
Instead of stone, your throne
a reclaimed tractor seat,
your staff a chiselled stick.
Working king, folk hero!

Do not be impatient
to bear the name my country gave me:
the title Living Treasure
means breathing
in a hinged glass box.

Do not be distracted
or your tomb will be empty,
a body beside no gifts.

Finally, do not look too much
to us, for treasure is
what imitates nothing else.
True kings discard influence.

Remember always to forget.
Only then can you be dug up,
held hard and shining to the light,
retrieved, alive as Culver,
and kick, kick, kicking.

The Potter's Daughter

In our house, a plate
was more than a simple dish.
        We ate
off your hardened hopes,
carried water in the heavy hold
of your conviction
that man could live off earth.

Steps to the cellar
sugared with red clay dust,
hair on your forearm
frosted with slip, our whole home
a showroom, wheel-hum
our lullaby, instead of bread
the brown smell
of canvas tabletops stained with work.

Your jugs and bowls
put food on our table.
For years I thought glaze
was your sweat,
a varnish of toil and love.

I was touched by your smooth hands,
their lines rubbed clean,
erased by years of circling grit.
Hands pulled from art
to practicality, our hungry
mouths calling you
craftsman, dish-seller,
until you were forced to answer.

Your hand, turning the sign
in the window after another
unvisited day, moved
with a despair of us, your untrimmable
offspring, as if we were flaws
discovered in the final firing,
sometimes the unpredicted
source of beauty, but more often
ruinous, incalculable errors,
forcing the same work
redone from the beginning.

When the bank finally came,
unsold ware hung on the shelves
like accusations: centuries of stone
may break into clay, but kilned porcelain
is a perfect survivor,
relentless testament to your skill,
to your fatherhood, to the perfect
shapes of failed attempts.

In the end, we learned patience,
a practised craft, as we watched
you waiting for our departure,
for time to begin again
setting other people's tables.

Before I step out the door,
I want to trace on your unreadable palms
a line that will remember
how when the money was gone
our cupboard was still not bare.

Glossary of Regret

Cobalt blue, aeolian bisque,
body frit,
                glaze.

Kiln at cone One.

                      Seconds
bearing blisters, raku.

Porcelain pug, soda ash,
         colemanite slips

bentonite slurry.

           White and red leads.
Slake.
              Talc.

Engobe lustre, crackle
kaolin.

Roll crusher, Two.
Ball crusher, Three.

Cone Four: fire. Egyptian paste.

Terra sigillata,

                    saggar. Blunge.

        Raku, tenmoku.

           Sgraffito shivering, rutile.

Cone Five, cone Six.

Vanadium,
   aventurine water glass.

       Minpro spar,
            majolica.

Seven:
Feldspar, water-smoking.

Catalysts

i

Fourteen years of laying brick
wore new lines into his hands,
on his palms a prosperous future
written in the wrong language.

On his shelves, the broken work
of youth long since replaced
by slip-mould dinnerware
and gift mugs with bitchy slogans,
store-bought symbols of treason
against abandoned ideology.
Even the nationalist, holding strong
dollars in his fist, might slip
across the border,
buy china in a shop.

A potter is the only worker
whose labour softens hands.
Calluses, rough landscape
of a foreign country, grown familiar.

ii

After fourteen years,
they searched for a new home
in the old quarter,
among the ruins of other lives,
walls that had withstood
cold marriages' dishes shattered
against them, had housed the Wedgewoods
bereaved children

bickered over, had sat wordless
beside the chamberpots of the dying.

All the houses looked the same,
empty as museum wings
between exhibitions,
the halls all hollowed
from the hope of change
scraping in opposite directions,
hope tracked in and out again
on newspaper paths laid down
over the carpets.

The kids appraised the clutter
lives collect.
His wife whispered, when you aren't at home
resist the urge to touch,
keep your hands to yourselves.

iii

In this brown bare box
of a house, the shell
of some other, duller bankruptcy,
a small temple.

On a mantel stood
a single blue vase, displayed.
In its foot, familiar initials
carved beside a date.
Fourteen years old.

His wife stepped back,
his children fell to their knees.

He took the pot and held it,
the weight of a planet.
The jar recollected his hands
on its thin hip, its cusped skin
fit his fingertips.
At the base, a spiral
from centre to rim, the trace
of his thumb's path.

The owner said, I'm afraid
I can't sell that, it's survived
all my life's disasters.
She laughed, as long as it is whole
I can't feel completely broke.
Besides, it is the only
piece of beauty I own.

iv

In his hands a whole blue world.
He returned it to its sad altar,
slowly, penitent
for so much already slipped
through his numbed, clumsy fingers.

In the car again, he reached out
to his wife's wet cheek.
Suddenly aware of the continuity
of surfaces, the error of naming places.
There is only time, measured in circles.

The world carries us on its skin,
spinning in stars innumerable as sand,
its soft heart callused with continents.

NOMADS

Offering

The vocabulary of desire
is incomplete, a word is missing.

My tongue searches
for your body in language
and finds you in every word.

I thought this was a small thing, a stone
in the palm I could offer you,
my body in darkness a simple gift
casual as a pebble.
As if touching were easier than speaking,
as if this poem did not prove you
inside me already, as if asking
meant I still had the power to invite.

But you make me aware of breathing,
of the awesome fact
that each particle of air
has been taken at least once
into every lung.
Suddenly I have no boundaries
and to kiss you seems to drink up the sky,
slip it from my tongue into your mouth.

Our bodies just our hearts' clothing,
and I came to you so shabbily dressed.
Maybe I thought that for one night
I could wear your beauty through closeness
and for a few hours believe myself
splendidly arrayed.

But you know all the lyrics
to rejection.
My body, your exquisite voice's
shattered glass.

The Rocks, Royal York and Lakeshore

This place was first yours, a break
in properties staked along the shore
where at the edge of an apartment lot, no cut path,
no cut step, you brought me late to the water's edge
to show me a whole Toronto,
the city as it is beheld each night
by headlights of cars pulling in one by one
to sleep by the lake's lip.

In a brief, almost invisible hesitation
the shoreline turns its face east,
casts a last furtive look toward the city,
its lost love,
as it moves along the arrow of southern Ontario,
pointed ever inward.

The tower blinks its red eyes every night
and proudly penetrates the sky,
a stubborn effort to forget the sight
of the lake's soft back, turned.

We would go down after dark
to the wet rocks, where waves licked
the hip of wounded land. Never
the same water twice, but all the water still leaving.
The secret place of last kisses, we would sit
and witness, over and over,
the precise moment of missing.

On warm winter nights a mist
hid mallards whose wings knew this little inlet.
Moon lost in milk, the late downtown lights
across the lake, gauze-clothed, struggled to be stars

to our gaze, and the ducks, just shadows
on the water's black flank, spoke sadly to us,
unseen, as though the sky itself sobbed.
The solemn rocks, the thin Humber, hard of hearing.

Sometimes the sky was cold and clear.
Toronto, distant and perfect – amber windows
sparkling, facets of yellow jewels reflected
in calm water – on those nights the city
wore the air tightly, a sheer black dress.
On those nights the lake paused, almost jealous.

Our walks always led here, to the black rocks.
We fed our love, deep jar of lake water, stones
and watched its level rise.
Somehow we displaced too much
and what splashed out was washed
back into the lake's rhythmic movement:
inward, inland, west.
Whatever it was, I went with it.

Your body is part of the landscape, the rocks
and your heart in geographic intimacy.
A place too permanent to offer forever,
even though the lake wishes
to take.

Hymenopterid Phenomena

Tonight you are thinking
of the puzzling architecture
of hornets, yellowjackets, and bees:
how their downy abdomens, striped
with black and yellow vees,
and little ochre helmets
are born construction warnings.

You remember reading somewhere
of the bees' dance:
how, with heavy wiggle, they can mime
the exact proximity of hive
to hidden gold mine of pollen.
Perhaps bees' bodies hold
a quantum knowledge, a buzz humans
cannot hear, because it hums
in a distant, sixth dimension.

                    Imagine!
Maybe for bees, six is everything.
Bees might be sixual creatures,
their sensuality, their whole busy society,
reflected in their hexagonal fabrications,
the same way a queer explanation of us
can be found in our erection
of minarets, towers, columns, spires.

Now you are thinking of your love,
how she loves honey.

Bone China

On a cushioned foot
stool embroidered
with flowers and legs
curving delicate
into paws of lions,
rests correctly
                a foot, unbound
unfolded from beneath
soft silk pointed
with trees and green
leaves, toes cringed.

How many years
she walked
on these clothed
fists.

I imagine her wanting
to step in sand,
to feel warm small
grains on skin
or to be

        simply
near water, close
to dolphins and fishes
who will love
her limbs, who share
with her shoes
the shape of tears.

Subic Bay

Nights, Kanos crossed
from the fenced-off base
into Olongapo.
We would wait for dates
in skiffs under the gatebridge,
in skin-tight skirts,
our sequins picking up
light off the fetid, used water.

Despite the guards who leered
from the road over the canal,
who shooed us away
like filthy strays,
we always stayed:
only early girls
caught the good boys' eyes,
landed ones who paid
with more than dinner.

Olongapo was always for
the Joes, from war
to war: in '44
the bay floor a final port
for scores of Nippon ships.
Then Korea's, then Vietnam's
back door.

We survived on rest
and recreation.
Mornings, we rinsed our panties
in the pipe-slowed
tears of Pinatubo.

~

Until the shamed
mountain's shoulders
trembled. A warning murmur,
two days before the hill's heart
swelled and burst.

Until Angeles was buried
while we hid among Manila's
tangled wires.

Until Olongapo stood, empty
as a midnight playground.
We returned to streets of dust,
raised black clouds at each step.
For months, we scrubbed
floors with the good soap of ash,
on dry days kids drew angels
in a dirty version of snow.

Until the army darkened
the recovering sky
with the black drone
of leaving reasons.

~

There is only so much
to remember.

My brother now cleans up
in Angeles, with his bare feet
maps whatever ash
winters leave unwashed,

tests the grey skirt of Pinatubo
each rain lifts bit by bit.

Tourists come to gawk
at rooftops gasping from the muck,
to walk the paths
where mud rivers waltzed
through sandbag walls.

He takes them up
a silt-choked stream,
wading through waters
still warm with earth's anger.
He walks ahead to scout
for quicksand, rolls up his pantcuff
to show his scalded leg:

they often tip in shame
to know it is his body
between them and a moving ground
still boiling
below the surface.

~

Dusk. I am back
at the gatebridge,
returned from the freeport
behind the fence,
where a suburb now grows
green lawns over ghost ground.
The base's secrets sold or guessed,
shotguns guard new investment
and artful gardens
sweet on volcanic talc.

These Kanos arrived
in courier planes, and packed
their wives. Above,
their cargo-heavy engines whine
white lines into the orange sky.

They call me *yaya*.
They pay me to keep up
with the dust.
Instead of Joes, I now amuse
executives' white children,
while downtown learns
a sobering way to entertain:
under tables, men play footsie
with our sooty little girls.

Blue jeepneys
circle by the guardbooth
as jewel-shelled beetles might shy
from a still boot heel.
Beyond the gate the bright
reflector-crusted bus
waits, rusting beneath the message
freshly painted on its roof:
Aim High Olongapo.

For twenty pesos
it will pick me up.
For twenty pesos, I can ride
those hope words home.

Test

It is not the loud sight of blood
that turns your head

as the nurse pricks your arm, pulls
two warm phials

of red, then caps and lays
the filled cylinders on a metal tray,

but the loss of you, offered
freely, as if your body could afford

to spend this much:
two tubes that strangely match,

in volume and diameter,
two severed fingers.

But blood grows back, like nails
or hair, and like the little tail

startled off a spotted gecko,
this sample is no

permanent amputation. Unless,
this time, the test

calls your hand, reveals
your casual gambling, your cells

risked like red chips. It is not
adultery, but getting caught

that costs. Once, in a back room
for a similar crime

a woman sat beside her husband
at a poker table, face turned

in shame: you pitied her debt,
a night calculated to one digit:

he had cut off her pinky.
Now, you think her lucky.

Miscarriage

The clot was born long before, in sleep. My womb
a makeshift welcome, long to warm, like the room
kept so clean, so well prepared, a guest is startling
and shocks the quiet air. The hard thing

is to see a cycle through, misnaming the orbit:
expecting the red bloom, to wait for it
watering as the shoot, having filled its own season,
closes and returns itself to earth. A reason

visits, hurries away with apologies. I wanted
to be disrupted, to be unable to unbend, haunted
by murmurs, blows, some stirring: but I am as whole
as a woman slept through a storm, told

in the morning of fierce thunder and struck trees,
who believes, but has nothing save the proof she sees
on waking: wet sidewalks, garden soil heavy with rain.
A scarlet flower between my legs. Maybe if pain

had announced the departure, waved like a gloved hand
in the window of a retreating train, I could stand
now suitably deserted, suitably empty, cradling my own
elbows in my palms. They said she had grown

for six weeks, quite normally, then stopped. I cried
at the terrible strength of my own desire. I tried
to remember another dream, besides this one fulfilled,
but my sleep's clothing was stained. I killed

her with a wish, as guilty as the blue sky. Freak
of nature, wilted instinct, leaky vessel. She was the weak
offspring I ate, piece by piece by piece. Where is the grief?
I dig for a missing body, unearth a strange relief.

Going Under

He is a doctor, full oathed to heal,
yet whose opiate hands hold the scale
where we, helpless, are weighed
against consciousness. Our will to feel
is heavy, anchors our bodies to pain.

He offers relief, can reel in the chain,
and set us briefly adrift on that sea
whose far shore, known
only to a hooded boatman,
we should never reach, loosed as we are
on his long lead, a leash
we hope will not stretch so far.

We are only leaving for a few hours,
a short sail – doctor's orders,
yet the heart rightly fears
any long trip,
knowing how time slips
away faster when real life
is on hold, and hopes he has set
some anachronism in our pocket
that will wake us back to land,
repaired and safe.

We kiss, then are wheeled away
into the night he measures, drop by drop.
He counts backward from ten,
I will see you again,
a valediction promising morning.

Teaching Mathematics

for Abe Shenitzer

X_I

Sometimes the human mind is beautiful
as numbers, perfect
as the thin matrix of grades
appearing slowly in my black book
as you learn.
Painting is colour's complex
calculation, and music
proof of sound's unsolvable theorems.
Numbers, more than words,
may speak the true God's name.

One hundred men's shut eyes
filled the room with darkness. I called out
in all our voices: a null thud
in the black air, damp with the sweat
and fear of old, sudden orphans.
We had seen our mothers and fathers
stand in single file, shivering, yet more still
than the best students of discipline;
at a glance I saw mine were two
of eight hundred and thirty six, that day.

I confess to no one: I am comforted
by the exactness of memory, in a present
full of uncancellable unknowns.

You still look to prove
what you already know.
Two hundred and six bones.

Six million years between 37 and 45.
The human mind:
the terrible precision of their books,
kept, as they were,
by starvation and loss.

X_2

Yet you must verify your marks.
For how can you have faith
in my ability to calculate
when I am but an incomplete equation,
the product of missing elements: my parents,
like the roots of negative numbers,
are truths I now only blindly believe in,
when I see how their omission
makes all one's answers turn out wrong.

Horses

We were the first four-by-fours,
muscular vehicles taming the land.
Flags cracked like whips in the west wind.
We ate out of your hands.

The tanned saddle's origin, the nightmares
of ground hooves kept us blind as motors,
ours the eyes of the ridden, your whores
who bridled silent, bucked at our own expense.

Instinct lived beyond your unbuilt fences,
was stampeded into the sea. But still our iron footfall
nailed smiles into the earth, patient
for steam, for sugar to fill our tanks,

and we thanked our flesh, that we could be broken
but not as machinery is broken,
that we would die unengineered, be well spoken
of, as the dead are.

We came to rest on oval courses.
We were driven by all that drives progress.
Forces.

The Silent Hall

for Ellen Betty King

The bell was not a bell
but a speaker, Ellen,

announcing what it should appeal:
our world's wagging tongue
has lost its fulcrum,

and cannot lift a word.

We left our names in your mouth,
but swallowed yours
and now can find nothing
to say.

The sky should have curved grey
over us, an iron bell
struck dumb by lightning's jagged crack,
but instead blinked brightly,
tears all wrung out.

Today we buried the voice
that spoke us.
Betty, our ears are burning.

Nomads

"In the Aral lies the people's destiny!"
  – Slogan on a wall in Muynak painted over in 1999

A killed sea is never swallowed,
no matter how the parched land drinks it down.

A killed sea is never buried, no matter
how often the turning hoe above
throws its clods of earth.

Salt, its white crushed bone, keeps rising.
Sea marrow crusts the fields, a rock-hard snow.

~

Our story, your story, has not been heard.
It has a thousand beginnings, only one end.

Born here, you know the sea only as legend.
A fishwives' tale, bloated with hyperbole.

Or worse, a dry history lesson,
a painting hung in the dim museum,
where varnish on the quay
slowly cracks, where fishermen's complexions
yellow.
The moral of all our parables,
its best illustration
is an empty page.

The Aral, a wreck sunk beneath sand,
a myth of ruin, a past evaporated.
Memory lost as a sailor to a sea burial.

~

It began over forty years ago
with the slow tapping of the Aral's veins.

The delusion of strangers to the desert,
clouds bursting out of sand.
In their dry mouths, a taste for power,
a craving for a thirsty crop.

Cotton ties off the long arm of the Syr Darya,
canals shunt the river's skin.
The Amu Darya is needled with pipes.
Like all dying things, the sea
must be drained completely
before it is embalmed in memory,

as if only a sea of dream could feed
an addiction to mirage.

You bend from the hips,
tilt your smooth head to the right
as if trying to read the spine
of a book on a low shelf,
part your lips to the pump's thin stream of water.

At fifteen, you've already bent a thousand times
over the field of tiny cloudpuffs.
The sack slung round your neck and waist
gapes like a mouth with your movement
as you pluck the bolls' grizzled heads
from their ravenous thorned throats.

In the cities, factories' loud machines
weave the long white shroud for a body
of water already turned to ghost.

~

To a sea, forty years fly fast
as a bullet. Forty years,
two generations of sudden death.

At whom will we point the finger
for pulling the stopper,
when Moscow, unflinching, escapes across a border
without fleeing an inch?
How can we wash our hands
when the crime is our empty sink?
Guilt may trigger

a wave of approved sympathy,
but one can't prove love
simply by paying for the funeral.

Here, the only just investigation
is memory. The only evidence:
anecdotes, tales,
dreams.

Forget, my son, and accuse yourself.

~

Each day carries the heavy fragrance
of the sea's burned body in the air,
the same salt smell of any harbour town.

Here the sea once lapped the shore.
From here, the tide rolled out and never returned.

Above us, geese are still free to pursue the seasons;
their arrow always points to spring.

They follow the wind that rippled
the reed forest, the bevel of wind
that ran through its wet green stalks
like an invisible comb through hair.
They chase the flight of beginnings,
the blooms that run up into the mountains
like small animals hunted by heat.

The Aral always was, as we once were, nomadic:
setting off from the snowfields of the Kush
it descended the wide paths of the Oxus and Jaxartes
to brave the Kara Kum.
It wore a different face in every land
but was stranger nowhere:
smiled in the mouth of a river,
cried from the eye of a storm.
While caravans bore their bolts of silk
from waterhole to waterhole,
the Aral was a mythic gypsy, laying down
an oasis
wherever it chose to rest,
and slept long in the arms of our country
before rising again into the clouds
that would return to the waiting summits.

Weary, the geese always paused here,
floated amid the tall flutes.

Now they find the marsh's long fingers
cut and yellow, lining the streets.
They perch on the town walls,
on knuckled bunches of reeds' hollow bones.

Now storms pick up the ash of dirty salt
from the sea's final resting place.
Bereaved, storms scatter it north

as far as Belorussia
and south over the glacier-tipped Pamirs,
as if the wind means to carry on
the sea's cyclical journey
while the desert oven
stubbornly continues its cremation.

They put an end to our wandering
to fill the fields with hands. All motion, arrested.

The sea only fled to escape being stilled.

~

The earth is exhausted, pumped up
like a Soviet athlete
on the steroid of abused water.

Dried stream beds pucker its fields,
the telltale stretch marks of unnatural growth,
while along the road trickles the yellow brine
of its chemical piss.

An old trained horse, the land knows only how
to run and drink, run and drink,
having learned the safety of blinders
when all its questions are answered
with whips.
Salt, a white foam
at the mouths of stagnant pools.

The memory of water blurs everything.
It is in the heat that turns the horizon to waves,
in the dark pools that form for an instant
on the blazing road, always in the distance,
always ahead of us, that evaporate as we draw near.

~

The monument to the Great Patriotic War
leans like the needle of a giant sundial
over a crumbling cliff, over the steep edge where the Aral
once precipitously began.
It points out toward the lone oil derrick
so distant you say it might be a minaret,
the speck of a lighthouse,
the bare flagpole of an anchored rig.

You read old slogans still visible
through the thin whitewash,
but can't remember the days before
statues of Timur sprouted like hardy weeds
all over the country, making monuments
out of hundreds of thousands of unnamed dead.

Statues of the sea, I know
are only a matter of time.

As a child, I dove from the memorial's tip
into the cupped palm of the sea.
The sea held me, thrilled and breathless, in blue
suspension, always guessing
at the texture of its deep floor
that my small feet could never touch.

Here.
Boats floated. Fish swam.
Water was pulled by the moon.

Now the monolith's dagger shadow falls
on lovers' cyrillic initials
traced in the sand or spelled with shells
for only the wind to wash away

leaving the sea floor like a secret
that should have never been revealed.

~

You take the cows out to the old harbour
to graze on brittle sagebrush
among the rusted carcasses of ships.
Frayed lengths of rope, black as your sister's braids,
lie coiled amid the thorny scrub.
Burned snakes in scorched grass, anchors' fossils.

This naval graveyard
has become a drinking place;
at night you and your friends climb onto the decks
to blur the stars with vodka. You pull the cork
as if hoping for a message,
but each time find your own call for rescue
washed up on this same shore.

Broken glass glints among bleached shells,
sharp sparks of bottle-green light.

Who knew our boats would become landmarks?
You pass first the little tugs that lean
toward a greenish pool; then farther on
some larger hulls stripped down to their curved ribs.
Rudders, never meant to be seen,
hang exposed above the sand – boats' vulgar genitals.
Then the trawlers, their empty portholes
the eye sockets of the dead.

At the farthest edge, at the brink
before the desert meets no more resistance,
lies my ship.

You run your fingers over the corroded shell;
the hull sheds its dull scales of rust.
You stand where I once did,
look back across the bow to naked vessels,
each tilted against a sandy dune
as though tossed on one last wave.

~

We are taught that only what is known exists,
a shared denial is a shared truth.
Slowly water retreats, replaced by ignorance.

Our truth is dust
swept under a Bukhara rug.

See how not seeing becomes no sea.
See how nothing to see becomes a shrine.

~

Dust says, I am like water.
I get into everything: through the small cracks
where walls meet, under windows' edges.
Into the corners of the eyes, under fingernails,
into the most private folds of skin.
Enter the world breathing water, leave it breathing me.

Your mother says her life is easier
because her small things are never stained:
her blood, thin as water, rinses clean away.

My hair smells like a broom.
A black tree, watered on dust,
grows in my lungs.

~

We have never heard of them;
they have never heard of us.

Karakalpak, our name like the sound
of white crystals under a boot heel,
or the fracture of dried reeds in the wind.

They call Muynak the edge of the world,
but even a land forgotten by the world
is a centre to those who live here,
the point around which our lives circle.
Here, too, noon follows morning,
night is stippled with the same constellations,
though nowhere else is the sun in the eye
so much like the glint of a badge.

~

Muynak's dawn is still tinged
with the corn-coloured light
of old propaganda films.

The wide streets are empty.
From inside the abandoned theatre,
the echo of sparrows.

"White gold" once shone in all our colours
like the sun behind stained glass.
Now young children confuse light with dust,
as each fights to fill the air
and shadows' grainy edges
struggle to remember the difference.

The spectrum of Muynak has grown thin.
Without rain our rainbow's bands
have shrivelled, tangled into a mess of brown.
Only your mother's bright dress and headscarf
sustain the memory of what it once was.
I have seen it, blowing past the town's mud walls
like a tumbleweed, or knot of hair.

The sacred hues of the sea
have become our god's name: unwritten on this land
and mocked in the stripes of the new flag
that whispers above our heads.

~

I don't remember how I saw the sea off,
the last time I dipped my hand in her waters,
wet my cheek with her salt tears.

The old men sit cross-legged on *tartas*
in front of the abandoned tea-house,
telling stories of the one that got away.
Praying, we pass our palms over our faces
as those who watched Noah recede into the distance
must have wiped from their eyes
the rain that hid their weeping.
The Aral grew more distant with each year.
But even when she turned her back to us
twenty miles from the docks,
we never believed she'd leave us forever.

I must have left the lapped shore
without one look over my shoulder,
perhaps even muttering some casual curse
in those final days when fishing
was a pointless argument with the sea,

like the last careless words to a loved one
who steps out on an errand
and never makes it home.

~

I miss waves. I miss
the sound outside my window
of the sea's moonlit breathing,
as a child breathes,
the rise and fall of its blue shoulders.

When I am gone,
let it be the sea that haunts you.
When the wind scatters you,
keep this story
like a seed in your mouth:
it has nowhere to grow
but your throat.

It is not the story
I wanted to leave you

but the one silence tells
ends much worse.

Winter Olympics

You've cut this satin costume
              all your life, traced the pattern in eights
of ice for eighteen years, until you grew
                   into this moment: a rink
made virgin just for your blade,
              the hushed congregation waits,
their cloudy breath wisping up like prayer,
                 your mother in her best pink

parka, pressing her mittened palms
                together, blinking back tears.
Suddenly, you worry about the faithfulness
             of thread: split seam,
loose hem, broken lace – you know now
             why the fiancée fears
not cold feet, but the torn sleeve, the stain.
            Do other girls dream

of a day like this, of spinning ice
            into a medallion of gold, of the world
allowing them, just once, to guess
           their own singular names? You could sew
tonight another star on your country's frayed
          red flag. Hair twirled,
lips frosted, eyes edged: you must pretend
         the judges aren't a row

of reluctant suitors, sixes
          tucked behind their backs like too-
expensive rings, until your body
         fulfills all its promises. Pretend they love
you, the waltz you've turned
        your ankle to by heart is your song, do

not let slip your own raised children:
                          axel, salchow, lutz. A voice from above

calls your name. Skate out
                          into the ellipse of light, opal of frost.
Freeze into the figure
                  of a cake-top ballerina, wait for the first note,
lift and offer your bare, unheld hand.
                          Before the music, history is paused,
your body fills the frame;
                  the audience huddles, pulling a heavy coat

of silence tight around its shoulders.
                          The song then bursts its corset strings,
melody, loyal partner
            through your youth's unending winter, rushes down
every aisle to meet you, to kiss
                  your feet, and like a scissor opening its wings
you step, cut the first curved slit
                  in the chaste, supine white sheet. Gown

of snow, slippers sharp
            as shards of glass, so many days as seamstress of one
sequined dress have earned this night
                          of stardom. Tonight, angels measure
your motion, refashion their flight.
                          Each leap, each arabesque, each run:
embroidery on your tight routine, recurring dream
                          of precious metal treasure.

So much is balanced on this thin edge,
                          on the path of a particle of light.
Did you forget some simple thing –
                  the church address, the priest, the ring?
A speck in the eye, a breath, a fall.
                          In an instant, your mother was right

all along: ice is a slippery lover. Futures
must be stitched with something

stronger: a finish line, or hoop, or net.
Pick up your shattered
body, as witnesses mourn
your torn smile. Finish the story each scratch
on ice once told, a fairy tale
with a cold end. As if love still mattered,
the rink is rose-littered, a red carpet
of bouquets you could not catch.

Ile-des-Chênes, Manitoba, 1996

We clasped our dry hands
and prayed
from our pockets,
tongues still parched
from last summer's drought.

Now we are answered,
chosen,
and the injured church walls swell,
plaster erupts, an acne of bubbles
breaks through paint.
Under granite, the water rises,
cement is heaved on the mud tide.
Wet stains wound
the thick cross of carpet,
spreading as fast as a bruise
blues the skin,
fast as the moon might open
into an eye of blood.
The angry river hurling away stones,
rising up under our feet
toward the grey sky.

Someone is documenting this
launching, like the ark,
of our house onto the giant lake,
new-born from the glutted river.
Our raft drifts amid poletops.
As we float, we pound our fists
on the boarded fourth-floor
windows within reach, yet
we are targets of another wrath
that won't be matched by sandbags

or our faith – when a storm
of cameras turns its eye, looks upon us
and is pleased.

Poseidon's mermaids drive the angels
from every bed's foot; the sea god
moves in. He reclines, uninvited
on our altar,
our rosaries and safes
swim among his locks, equally weightless
under the flood's blind hand –

as I am now, ascended
above his newly conquered city, I see
as gods and other viewers must,
the even similarity
of rooftops, sad shingled pyramids
rising out of a watery desert.

An almost perfect, level moment.
True fairness' empty scape.

Somewhere far-away there are televisions,
doorsteps, graves still resting under the earth, a place
where gravity still exists.
A solid heaven where someone sits
and watches, confirmed in his belief
that nature's commandments have proclaimed
him the righteous, and us

the drowned, the unconfessed,
the guilty.

Referendum

with sincere apologies to Gilles Vigneault

Of course, you want your country
to be one long season,
when snow hides the dark mud,
when nothing moves and nothing grows,
when the white sky and white land agree
to dissolve the horizon *à la lointaine*, and one
can judge no distances.

The treachery of spring, when the land
changes colours, the leaves are turncoats,
and the rippling fields
are stripped of their sheets
and wait to be stained with seed.

You are waiting for another winter,
when the fleur-de-lys' white petals
will cover the earth in a garden of snow,
the cold air will remain cloudless,
free of the visible breath of spoken h's,
and your swallowed aspirations
will take root in your body and grow
out of your mouth, watered by a clean tongue.

Ton pays est une frontière
ineffaceable, une cicatrice dans la terre,
dont la terre ne se gêne pas
parce qu'elle est portée
sous un manteau de castor, sous une ceinture
flechée.

Here, what have I proven? All depends
on where you're coming from.

My country is not your country of snow,
Mon pays, ce n'est pas un pays, c'est ma peau.

Roti, Manitoba

The red round fell into the fields
and we lit the kitchen first,
yellow room against the swollen sky.
Outside, wheat shoots lost in darkness
leaned toward the dusk sun of our window.

She sent me for the heavy bowl,
chipped and cool from the cupboard,
for pin, plate, and *tahwah*.
Over the element's red circle,
she melted butter, ghee's imposter,
in an earthen cup
while my small hands softened the counter
with flour.

Flour and warm water, dough tacked
like gum to our powdered fingers,
she worked the white dust in, until
the bread flesh came away:
round as breasts, pale and smooth as skin
I'd never have, but imagined.

Rolled flat, butter-rubbed,
folded, balled, and rolled again,
roti was our only ritual.
I asked about a white dress, practised
the refrains of Communion,
while she cast water on the oiled iron,
let me watch the droplets hop.

Heat freckled the flat bread, the moon
saw its surface rise from the stove.
Until the moment

only she knew how to wait for,
to steal it, thin and sizzling, from the *tahwah*
and clap it quick and soft between her palms.

After curry, she shook her head
as I spread peanut butter on the last roti.

I ate and only noticed I was shivering
when she leaned to close the window
against the strong Canadian wind,
growing stronger.

Going Back

Cyan sky, swan's blue.
Sun so high and sharp, clouds
cut clean shadows over the lake.

Looking out from the crowded car
as we fly north,
bare feet on the dashboard,
hand palm down out the window, wrist loose
undulating in the cool airstream
like a goose's long neck.

This far north, sun competes
with the trees, forest
thick as a flock. Pine green dark,
greedy for all the light.
Colours mark territories in broad strokes:
sky, road, trees, lakes.

Suddenly, startled by our speed,
bats' cluttered flight:
scraps of night blown like litter
across the day, a flutter of black paper.

Time travellers can't trust sight,
must navigate blind.

~

Along the highway, cut layers of shield,
millefeuille of rock.
Road curve, the lip of a plate.

Grandmère, this is the same road
my parents must have followed
to reach you, to ask for permission
they had already taken.
Me, still a guess inside her.

Pulled north at eighteen,
she arrived with a suitcase for two weeks,
stayed a lifetime.
Even now, my mother can't pass granite
without admiring its thin striations,
the patience with which it laid itself down
skin by skin.

The magnetism of land, of bodies,
impossible to tell apart.
Repulsion, like attraction,
can throw us together, can keep us there.

~

An artist's child, an early awareness
of colour.
I pointed to every black man
on television, asked why
he wasn't my father.
Why brown was black; pink, white.
Why no one called me grey.

I learned to look not at the object
but for the curve of space that holds it,
for the simple shapes that build
complexity.

She said art was a struggle
with form, to produce a challenging beauty.
Only now do I understand
she was talking about their marriage.

A child of artists, my hand saw a body
as a dynamic collection
of cylinders, trapezoids, spheres.
                              But their story
trained my eye
against the illusion of wholeness,
to see in bodies the many bodies,
the simple parts each body chooses,
the combination of elements.
Complexions.

Even then I knew
there are no such things
as primary colours.

Only light, and surfaces.

~

We pass through Rouyn.
All the low, wood-sided houses
tilt toward the river, as though the town
thinks itself meant for the harbour.

Your old home is sixteen miles out
on unnamed lanes, farms for landmarks.
You point to a rise in the field
that for eight months of the year
snowbanks hide from the gravel road.
You remember it. It's still there.

My father's name was pronounceable here,
where his grandfather once blasted rock
to lay the foundation of this house.
When he lost his accent,
you said a part of this place went with it.

When she lost hers, congratulations,
though certain words she almost spoke
with a mouth full of *pure laine*!
"Tree" no longer a number,
"fate" transformed to "faith."

Thirty years later, still
no one in this town expects
brown grandchildren.
I arrive speaking a travelled tongue.

This far north, they say,
is snow country:
all year light falls at the same cold angle,
the land only welcomes those born on it.

~

The church hall reunion, the same profile
sketched onto three hundred faces.
My mother, unmistakable in the corner
a picture of difference.
She sits next to you, another woman
who has yet to return to where she was born.

This is another moment
when colour joins us, sets us apart.
No matter where I stand in this room,
I am her daughter

until someone touches my shoulder,
il faut que tu sois un Ledoux:
that nose, those eyes, a bit of mouth.

I am recognized.

~

On the drive home, without warning
the signs change their language.
The cold morning keeps the windows up.

Frames forget movement,
insist on opposites.
They forget that the shore
is both sea and sand,
that the sky is light and water.
Even night and day meet each other
at the limit that is beauty, give themselves up
to colour, indistinguishable in the moment
of joining.

I once painted the sky
as a stripe at the top of the page,
until my parents said the sky
falls right down to the ground, has no edges.

The highway stretches out.
I close my eyes against the new day
but light seeps through skin. I doze
as my father tells the same old story:
before her, he never knew his eyes
were the green of mangoes.

This car, time traveller.
We drive home,

the exact distance of our past.
Grandmère, have you been listening?

Trees still line up at the road's edge:
stubborn as green cadets against
the changing seasons.
Layers of rock, still patient.

We are in the sky.

CHEJU DIARY

Haenyo Song: Morning

Wind tugs at the water's surface,
tries to peel back its skin.

Water stretches across the filled shallows
like cellophane over an earthen bowl:
waterboatmen skid on its film,
sandgrebes float, imperceptibly suspended.

Each morning our bodies melt through
the water's thin defence.
Our work a daily osmosis, we are accepted
by the membrane's invisible pores.

Waves, regular as heartbeat.
Sand flutters like the skin at the wrist.

We test the sea's pulse against our limbs,
then dive in, and swim the rocky hollows –
our bodies carried in water, pushed like blood
through the earth's aorta, its ventricles.

At dusk, the sea exhales us.

Foreigners

Our first lesson is separation.

Men in one car, women in another,
we drive into the unfamiliar.

I mistake an *orum* hill
for the mountain, until mist lifts
to reveal the horizon's true height. Halla

and Sea always facing each other,
a proper old couple, silent,
faithfully keeping to themselves.

Banners strung between pines
coil in the wind, sling
triplet fistfuls of Hangul,
a stick and pebble alphabet.

Surrounded by this language
I cannot read, these strange letters
are silk-swathed stones
that hit the eye without touching,
that leave a slow pain
but no bruises.

Only loneliness.
The first lesson.

We speed into the wordless
landscape.
Hurtling stasis, a year or two
will pass like these first glimpses,
at the startling speed
of staying the same.

Haenyo Song: Warning

Today, the first bombs fell on Belgrade
and their sky wears that same bruised shade

of grey, that one outside over forty hues
between blue and blackness fused

in the diving woman's rainbow, that warns
a coming storm not of weather but born

from men's windfilled hollows. The sky is a sea
where the whale of power swims silent,

dark as a cloud and just as benevolent,
where we, little fish quailing in shadow, see

nothing but hungry underbelly. I know
all the sky's chameleon colours: rinsed indigo

after the day's typhoon — like Hanbok's damp silk,
sailors' azure, snow-filled maroon, the milk-

blue promise of sun and good harvest. But that grey —
solid as a battleship's flank, the distant quay

trembled by waves — the sky was a stranger,
a new uniform hiding its face. The sun

torn off and lost like a loose button. Danger
hums in any light outside our spectrum —

in infrared stealth, in ultraviolet burn —
but I couldn't hide; my naked eye saw

all that the sky's new clothes exposed: the raw,
shameful wound of its premonition, and learned

the terror in its dark silence,
in its camouflage attempt, the animal defence.

Cursed with vision, I saw through skin
the knobbed white bones of clouds. I hoped never again

to see the sky so stained. It took five years
to soak it out, and traces still remain: fear

still tinges the water, the receding tide
leaves its wet shadow on the sand. Memory hides

in our bodies: each morning we dive, bury
ourselves in the sea, but memory won't drown.

The dead's empty bellies fill us. We resurface.
Look to the sky: our hunger won't stay down.

Mok Sok Wan

What kind of garden is this?
Piles of rubble, rocks behind glass,
some propped-up dead wood.

Without names, we feel cheated by stone;
helpless in a mute museum.

A word in English changes everything:
this root, the horsedragon's twisted sinew,
suddenly the movement of reincarnation
in the rock's striated muscle.

One man's imagination
translates the ideograms of a frightened island:
he bent close and heard in the petrified shape
of roots the long memory of lava,
whose crest like a hot blade shaved
the forest to stubble,
razing the thick fur of pines
to a skin of scorched earth. Melted rock
beading between stumps like spilled mercury.

Roots with these names:
wanting wings, broach
of commandment, eyes
stretching ambition.
Walking virgin forest, triumphal
tree. The poised skeletons of waves
must look just like this.

With her hands, a blind woman reads
an expression on that rock's face.
On that weedy patch, a legend of marriage
is told by pebbles.

Oh – the gate is closing,
move with the busloads out to the lot.
From there, you can see

the loud red azaleas, the tangerine
groves, the yellow
rapeflowers patching the fields,
and along the highway, unopened dandelions
nodding from milky stems
like straw-filled horsejaws on jade necks:
cacophonous colour, so often sung.

"Amazing how stones hold so much
in silence."

Tol Harubang

Porous surface of basalt,
of pestle, bowl, and grindstone
sharing the shaman altar's
coarse face, its pocks
volcanic birthmarks,
        great-grandfather:

lone sentinel
beside the even cedar galebreak
beside the jagged wall
piled of broken rock:
the stone man folds
his hands, his hard stare
gathers the gateless island.

Beyond the three-dowelled
doors, the cottage roofs'
roped and cobble-weighted thatch –
the mountain, beyond it
the black beach,
the wind-swept strait, the sea.

His senseless eyes
can't close.
Stone-deaf, he hears
with his pores.
Nothing surprises him

but the children who
still smart drum skin
with his name:
tol, tol, tol, tol.

On their little cheeks,
a star-mark fades.

He is our spirits' witness —
solemn, mute, amused.

For him, this alliterative music.

Settlers

Eight dry days, and each morning
a thick yellow dust
settles a skin on every surface:
when the wind stills, azaleas
pretend to be daffodils,
and aspiring oranges get their taste
of life as a grapefruit.
Even evergreens steal a moment
of false fall colour.

I write my name
on the arm of the chair by the window,
on flat leaves, on shelves,
on an old mirror discarded
in the empty stairwell:
my reflection in the glass
is the powdered face
of a girl grown into a woman's rules.

I always thought "yellow" an epithet,
but it is a word they gave themselves.
Maybe to them I am prettier
unwashed.

Not just lost skin, this dust
is pollen, lifted from pines
by the breeze. The forest
smells like a lovers' bed. Don't ask
the horticulturists
for details by day,
they are too busy
building a better orange.
At night, they will tell you

of the yellow sands of Mongolia
carried by wind over the sea,
and how their ancestors once followed.

At last, the rain.
The stippled puddles
are ringed with yellow froth.
In little rivulets, lemony tendrils
curl toward the drains.

My trace rinsed from surfaces.
Skin I won't see again.

Haenyo Song: Harvest

We cull the island's most spectacular fields.

Cheju's long grasses have always belonged to the women.
Like our inland sisters who crouch in flocks
along the roadsides, cutting and tying
tall stalks into bundles,
we too wrap our heads in white towels, and bend to trim
the jagged underwater lawns.

We envy the sun's long arms, its deep reach.
Crystals of light collect on the sea floor,
settle like sugar in a glass of water, dusting
the greedy seaweed fronds. When stirred by our fins,
light disperses, dissolves. It clings to our bodies.
We swim, pollinating the watery garden.

Other crops move in the wet meadow: we hunt
mobile vegetables – cucumbers with fingers,
flowers with feet!
The urchin flees, millimetres per minute,
on its single, toothed paw. The sola retreats
into its white turban, tries to pass for one of us.
The conch shies from the hand, curls into itself
as a bud cringes before it is picked.

~

Eighty-nine fires lit on Halla.

Nagasaki, Hiroshima: dropped
casually as pebbles into a pond,
but the ripples lashed our shores for years.

Spread on their dissection table,
Korea was a little rabbit
on a stranger's map,
dangling in China's paw or snagged
in the hind claw of Russia

if they had cared to look:
they performed their secret operation
blindfolded, in a far-away room,
the paper decision to sever its head
as easy as unpinning
a drawn donkey's tail.

Everyone forgets islands
but the armies.
Cheju, both their rabbit's foot
and a dropping at its heel.
Our own country
gnawing us off at the ankle
to escape.

~

What the sea gave back freely moved us first:

He bobbed up, his pale back
a bullet-pitted coral,
shreds of skin around the wounds
like the red blooms of anemone's flower.

His mute body told the whole story,
the exact cost of silence –
two blunt stumps announced his lost thumbs;
his tongue, waterlogged and swollen with secrets,
tumbled from the cave of his mouth,
dumbstruck as the long-hidden survivor
who emerges from the dark shelter, and stumbles
into the sober, devastated day.

My own child in the basket
beside the water, among the fishbaskets
and waterjugs. A boy disguised
as part of our harvest.

~

The stories from Orari, from Bucholi,
of black stones soaked in red.
Suddenly, blood oranges.

Hatred is a crafty child,
who finds even in a farmer's field
torture's toybox:
who needs weapons when at hand
is onion's green-tailed whip,
the rape-efficient orange root,
and the killstone of white radish?

Every war has its gory theatre
it forces the land to watch.
Cruelty laughing at the same joke
over and over.

The stories from Gyoraeri.
From Oradong.

Eventually we all marry those
who killed our parents,
and call it peace.
This is how I know the North
is not lost to us forever.

~

Land's memory
is so much longer
than water's.

Graves rise from clearings on the *orum*,
the small hills helmet the dead.
When rapeflowers grow bright
on the little mounds, they sleep
curled like children beneath a yellow blanket.

The trees remind me of fear:
hack them to stumps; still, deep roots
stay tangled underground.

The sun says nothing, recedes
as if its radiant face would offend.
We walk in the timid light
that filters through the gauze of cloud
bandaging the island, afraid
to scar the soil with our shadows.

~

I am full of lessons I cannot share:

How wild grass cleans the mist
from goggles, how to hook the sicklecord
at the elbow, not the neck.

How to find feather stars and sea lilies.
The flounce of scallops, sea slugs' ruffled skirts,
the split gourd shape of cuttlefish.

How the concave of the abalone,
its hard slick of colour, is like the skin
of gasoline on water, a liquid prism.

The depth of crab and shrimp. The myth
of sand dollars, the bottle mouths of sea squirts.
Polyps. Molluscs.

How we learned to respect
their reluctance to leave, the bravado of shells.
How we learned to love
the sea's slow resistance.

Cheju

The east wind billows the Korean peninsula, a sail
disoriented, finds west. This island, little hull, a pebble

anchor. Its currency of oranges, changing hands
as ginkgo leaves fall, a traditional dance's discarded fans,

as hotels watch suns rise heavily from the ocean, sentinels
over the finned bodies of women diving for shells,

the squid boats extinguishing their lights,
one by one, dying fireflies on the water: mirror of night's

retreating stars. Our fingers smell of broken skin,
of mandarins shining in fists, like coins.

Trail-wounded, stitched with wooden stairs, the mountain
rolls down its windworn cheek a rain

which only wants to meet the sea. It will be caught
in groves' soil, thirsty for tears, a perfect net.

Where we have confused boats for land, fruit for gold.
The above country catches the now, the current.
What this hull, this pebble anchor, will hold.

Epilogue: The Moth's Lesson

Once I read of a moth
accidentally closed
inside the flat half-bell
of a grand piano,
the eerie counterpoint
of random notes struck
by frantic wings,
the strange, asymmetrical
tones of its struggle.

Long silences broken
with gasps
of futile music. Longer silences.
Then the beautiful cacophony
before the strings' final,
dying vibrations
became still.

A silly waste, I thought,
simply a matter of waiting
for a hand to lift the lid.
The moth chose instead
to play, against the soft felt
of its body, a requiem.

A moth does not expect
to make a noise on earth.
It is the price of weightlessness
that wings must be content
to barely whisper air.
Still, the moth has a purpose:
born believing in destinies,
its body burns

to throw itself into fire,
and lives
its whole life striving
to become one with light.

What were its choices?
Hours or years might pass
before the hollow darkness broke,
before a passing wind bent back
the piano's hinged black wing,
a release completely ignorant
of its prisoner.
Patience, tamed and quiet, for chance
to open into chance.

A contemplation of ash,
of a singed body in a dustbin, perhaps,
or else its missing witnesses
dimmed the flaming
image of a moth's noble death,
the bright star it had followed,
illuminated only the pointlessness
of believing in but one path
to the end, that in the end
is the same for all.

We rush toward absence,
a finish cheered by stones.

I understand that moth.
What we make of living
is remembered only by the living.
The only joy of trying
is to listen
for its brief, absurd music,
and if you are brave enough to hear it,
dance.

Notes on the Text

"Hiatus"

Bernard Leach (1887–1979) is widely recognized as one of
the most influential figures in the studio pottery movement.
Introduced to pottery during his travels in Asia, Leach's
meeting with Japanese potter Shoji Hamada (declared a
"national living treasure" in his own country) led to a his-
toric collaboration that saw the two men found the St. Ives
pottery in Britain, effectively transporting the Korean and
Japanese workshop practices to the West, and establishing an
aesthetic tradition that would influence younger potters for
generations afterwards.

"Nomads"

The Aral Sea is one of the world's largest inland seas and is
located in Uzbekistan, a former Soviet Republic. Over the
last forty years, the shoreline has receded more than one
hundred kilometres and the sea's surface area is now half its
former size. This environmental disaster is the result of the
diversion of river water for large-scale irrigation, and con-
tinues to worsen. The severe health problems of local resi-
dents are one of the world's most graphic examples of the
physiological effects of environmental damage.

"Subic Bay"

In 1900, the Americans built a naval station at Subic Bay,
about forty kilometres northwest of Manila. The Japanese
fleet was defeated there during the Second World War, and
the base saw the height of its activity during the Vietnam War.
The town of Olongapo became home to the 7th Fleet of the
U.S. navy, and its economy relied heavily on supporting

the Americans' professional and recreational activities. In 1991, the navy pulled out when the Philippine government refused to extend an agreement that allowed the U.S. to use the bay. Their leaving coincided with the June 1991 eruption of Mt. Pinatubo, perhaps the planet's worst volcanic outburst of the century.

"Cheju Diary"

The island province of Cheju-do lies eighty-five kilometres off the southernmost tip of the South Korean peninsula, and owes many of its cultural distinctions to its geographic and social isolation from the mainland. A favourite honeymoon spot for Korean newlyweds, the island now promotes itself as "the Hawaii of Asia" and touts the few women that still work as divers as a main attraction. Not mentioned in the tourist literature are the events that took place from 1948–1953, when Cheju's political opposition to the division of the country and to the elections taking place on the mainland was brutally suppressed during a period of American occupation. Referred to as the April 3rd massacre, it is estimated that between 40,000 to 80,000 people (nearly a quarter of the island's population, and most of them civilians) were tortured and killed by South Korean troops reporting to American officers.

Acknowledgements

"Hiatus" first appeared in the *Malahat Review* and was a co-winner of the 1999 Long Poem Prize, and an earlier version of "Nomads" won the 2000 Bronwen Wallace Award competition. Some of the shorter poems were part of an earlier manuscript entitled "A Strange Relief," which was shortlisted for the 1998 League of Canadian Poets Chapbook Award and was a finalist for the 1999 Shaunt Basmijian Award. "Winter Olympics" first appeared in the *Malahat Review*.

First, thanks to my family – Jason, Janet, Tanya, and Jordan L'Abbé – and to Jerome Shaw.

Thanks to Ian Small, Michelle Oser, and Lola, without whose great help "Nomads" could not have been written. Thanks to Tim Conley for his friendship and his unmatchable commitment to language. Thanks to each one of my friends for their emotional support, their critical honesty, and for just being there to enjoy the ride with me, especially Courtney Harris, Carlos Salvador, Alan Edwards, and Scott McLaren.

Thanks to the many people who read my work with such close attention and who offered invaluable encouragement: Austin Clarke, Janice Kulyk Keefer, Constance Rooke, Pierre L'Abbé, Allan Briesmaster, Mary Ellen Csamer (for "Cheju"), and Marlene Cookshaw. Thanks of course to Molly Peacock for her guidance and to Ellen Seligman for her receptiveness and enthusiasm.

Thanks to the Ontario Council of Arts for its assistance and to the editors at Brick Books and *Arc Magazine* for their recommendations on my behalf.

Finally, I am indebted to all those whose voices and struggles I've presumed to represent in some of these poems. I hope this work has heard you.